W9-CSL-316

To Canada, our home

C1
KV
Sep 95
16.95

THANKSGIVING DAY
IN CANADA

by Krys Val Lewicki

illustrated by Ana Auml

Napoleon Publishing

Irene and her older brother Richard could hardly wait. They had known about it for a week now and here they were!
The car pulled into the driveway.

After big hugs and then some more, Mom and Dad announced, "We can unpack later.
Right now we're going to the market to get a few things for tomorrow's Thanksgiving dinner."

Richard's eyes sparkled like shiny new Canadian dollars as he ran up to his Mom. "Can I come along to get the turkey? I'm pretty strong and Dad might need some help."

"Maybe you should," agreed Grandpa, and soon all that could be seen was Richard's black cap waving as the car disappeared over the hill.

Entering the house, Irene ran ahead of her grandparents to say hello to Bonbon, the goldfish she had given them for Christmas.
"Are you excited about tomorrow?" asked Grandma as they settled down in the living room.
"Oh yes," Irene replied, "...only...why do they call it Thanksgiving Day?"

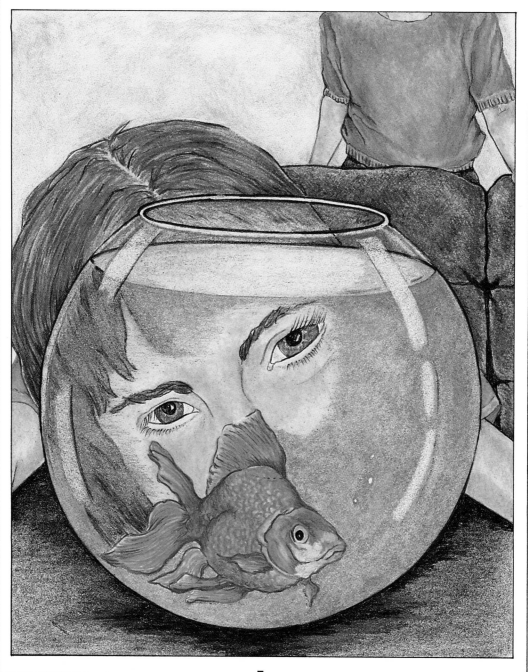

Grandpa looked up at Grandma and gave her a wink. She smiled back and said, "You go ahead, dear. I'm going into the kitchen."
Then Grandpa got up, cleared his throat and started to tell the story...just as all Grandpas do.

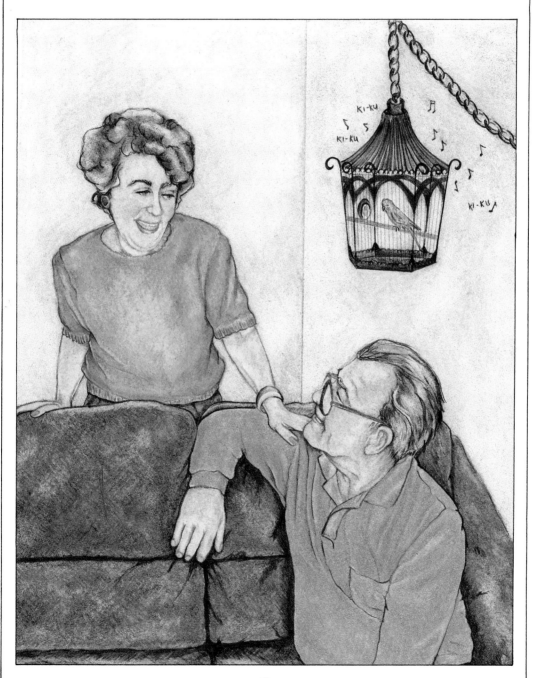

"Well, you see, there are three traditions behind our Canadian Thanksgiving Day.
Long ago, before the first Europeans arrived in North America, the farmers in Europe held celebrations at harvest time.

To give thanks for their good fortune and the abundance of food, the farm workers filled a curved goat's horn with fruit and grain.
This symbol was called a cornucopia or horn of plenty.

Irene, do you know where the first North American Thanksgiving took place?" asked Grandpa.
Irene shrugged her shoulders as Grandpa pulled out some old books and continued.

"Way back in the year 1578, the English navigator Martin Frobisher held a formal ceremony, in what is now called Newfoundland, to give thanks for surviving the long journey.

He was later knighted and had an inlet of the Atlantic Ocean in northern Canada named after him–Frobisher Bay.

Other settlers arrived and continued these ceremonies. That was the second influence on Thanksgiving.

FIRST ENGLISH THANKSGIVING HELD ON NORTH AMERICAN SOIL

The third came in the year 1621, in what was to be the United States, when the Pilgrims celebrated their first harvest in the New World. The Pilgrims were English colonists who had founded the first permanent European settlement at Plymouth, Massachusetts, a year earlier.
It was an historical Thanksgiving, mixing the usual harvest ceremonies of the local Indian Chief Massasoit and his Wampanoag tribe, with

those of the Pilgrim settlers and their leader Governor Bradford. This harvest festival helped to introduce the new settlers to foods such as American wild turkey, cornbread, squash and pumpkin.
Even the kids had fun picking wild cranberries from nearby bogs and munching on corn that was roasted, popped and covered with maple sugar.

In the 1600's, French settlers, having crossed the ocean and arrived in Canada with explorer Samuel de Champlain, also held huge feasts of thanks. They even formed "The Order of Good Cheer" and gladly shared their food with their Indian neighbours.

In the 1750's, American settlers from the south brought their joyous celebration to Nova Scotia. After the Seven Year's War ended in 1763, the citizens of Halifax held a special day of Thanksgiving.

Those Americans who remained faithful to the government in England were known as Loyalists. At the time of the American revolution, they moved to Canada and spread the Thanksgiving celebration to other parts of the country. Many of the new English settlers from Great Britain were also used to having a harvest celebration in their churches every autumn.

Eventually, in 1879, Parliament declared November 6th a day of Thanksgiving and a national holiday.

Over the years, later and earlier dates were used for Thanksgiving–the most popular being the 3rd Monday in October.

Then, after World War I, the war in which your great-grandfather fought," said Grandpa, "both Armistice Day and Thanksgiving were celebrated on the Monday of the week in which November 11th occurred. Ten years later, in 1931, the two days again became separate holidays and Armistice Day was renamed Remembrance Day.

Finally, on January 31st, 1957, Parliament proclaimed...

   'A Day of General Thanksgiving to Almighty God for the bountiful harvest with which Canada has been blessed,'
...to be observed on the 2nd Monday in October.

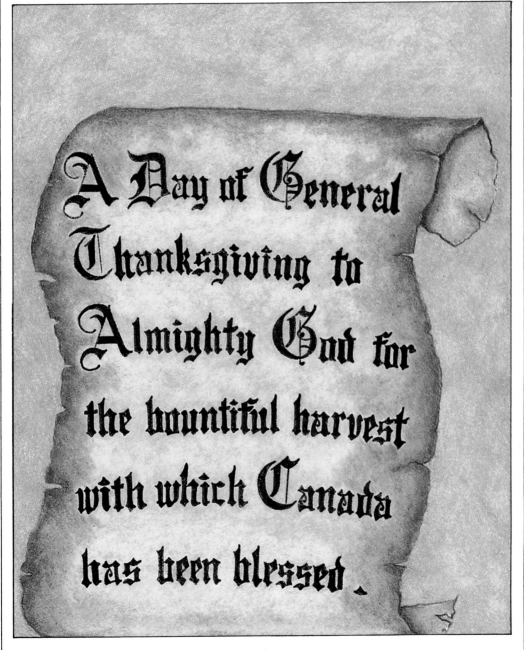

Our American neighbours live to the south of Canada where in most places it stays warmer for a longer time and the harvest is later. They observe Thanksgiving on the 4th Thursday in November, according to a law passed by President Abraham Lincoln in 1863.

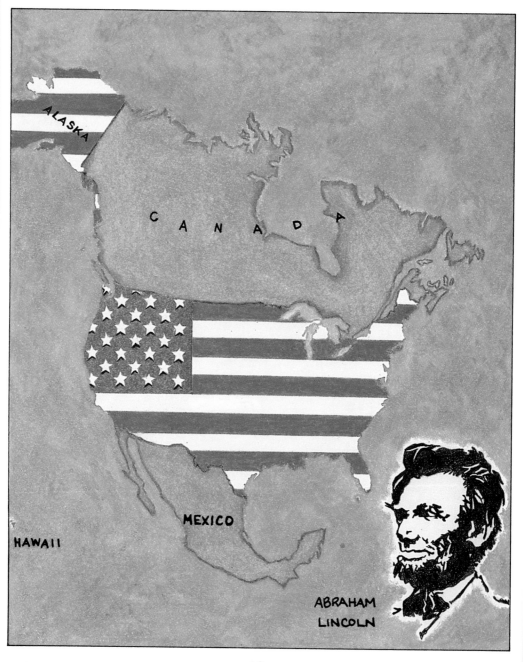

And there you have it," said Grandpa proudly, "the history of
Thanksgiving Day in Canada."

"How about some freshly made cookies?" asked Grandma as she entered the room. "And here's some tea for Grandpa and milk for you, dear."

"Mm-hm-hmm, these are terrific, Grandma! Where did you learn to bake like that?" asked Irene, reaching for another cookie.

"Well, dear," replied Grandma, "when I was a little girl, Thanksgiving was a very special time...a time of tradition. I was about your age and we lived out on the farm. It was the 1920s and we didn't even have a refrigerator," said Grandma. Irene's mouth opened in amazement.

"The night before Thanksgiving Day, Mother would begin the preparations. While I helped to roll the dough for the pies, she would bake the bread and start boiling the cranberries and apples for the sauce.

All the pies, whether pumpkin, apple, pecan, raisin or maple sugar, would be baked and left to cool on the window-sill overnight.

Meanwhile, Father prepared the cider and then, at midnight, would make a big fire in the stove so it would be good and hot for the next day.

The following morning we would go to pick fresh vegetables. I would always stay close to my Mother as we neared our garden patch.

DOROTHY LYNAS

That was because I was a little afraid of the big scarecrow who seemed aware of everything that approached its field.

Later on, a neighbour would come by in a big hay wagon and take all the children on an exciting, fun-filled ride through the autumn-coloured countryside.

At home," Grandma continued, "Mother had put the turkey into the oven. There was no room left on the stove as many, many pots boiled and sputtered. The delicious smells soon reached every corner of our hungry house. To keep the stove going, Father would bring in another bucket of freshly chopped wood and leave it by the old straw broom.

Meanwhile, as some of the vegetables cooled, Mother readied the candied yams, mashed potatoes, gravy, creamed onions, squash, jelly and sometimes even wild rice.

Then she would take the dry sage, which hung from the ceiling by a string, and crush it by hand or in a bowl called a mortar, using a stick-like pestle. Herbs were added to the bread and onions to make our favourite...the stuffing!

The celebration was always a time of family...
a time of sharing
and giving thanks."

Irene hugged Grandpa, then she jumped from the couch and ran over to hug Grandma too.

They heard the car returning.

Irene could hardly contain herself. She ran out the door shouting, "I know all about the history and tradition of Thanksgiving Day!"

Grandma and Grandpa stood together by the living room window. They smiled as they watched Richard helping his parents and Irene running around excitedly telling everyone what she had learned. The celebration had begun.
It was going to be a wonderful Thanksgiving.

The Canadian Thanksgiving Song

Music and Lyrics by Krys Val Lewicki

Lively, Brightly (♩ = 96)

1.) The har - vest ce - le - bra - tion __ first
2.) Oc - to - ber paints a land so green with

sailed a - cross the sea, it filled our folks with love and hope in the new world co - lo - ny.
yel - low, orange and red, we take this chance to give our thanks __ for fami - ly, home and bread. An

Fro - bi - sher, __ Chief Mas - sa - soit, __ the Pil - grims and Cham - plain, they are why we're gath - ered here and
a - ges old __ tra - di - tion, __ still car - ried on to - day, Our na - tion's heart will ne - ver part, if

sing - ing this re - frain. As the leaves go dan - cing 'round and 'round and 'round __ they play, In
we be - lieve this way. And

Ca - na - da __ we ce - le - brate our Thanks - gi - ving day. We ce - le - brate, __ we ce - le - brate, __ we

ce - le - brate __ to - day, in Ca - na - da __ we ce - le - brate our Thanks - gi - ving day. With

---

35

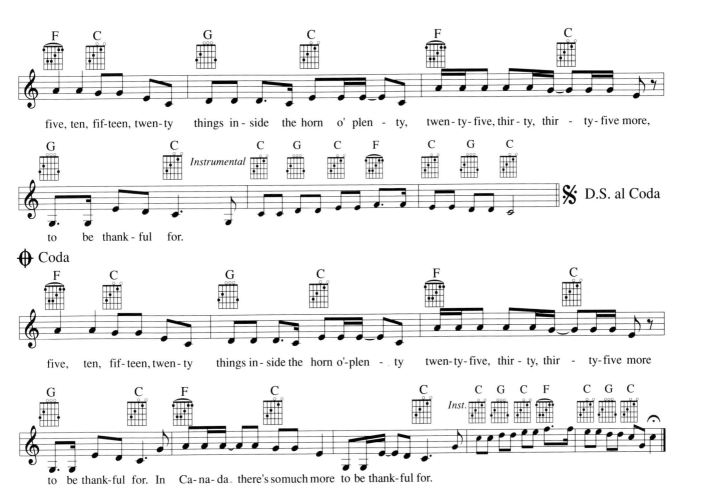

five, ten, fif-teen, twen-ty   things in - side   the horn   o' plen - ty,   twen-ty-five, thir - ty, thir - ty - five more,

Instrumental   **D.S. al Coda**

to   be thank - ful   for.

Coda

five,   ten,   fif-teen, twen-ty   things in - side the horn o'-plen - ty   twen-ty-five, thir - ty, thir - ty-five more

Inst.

to   be thank-ful for. In   Ca - na - da   there's so much more to be thank-ful for.

1.) The harvest celebration
    First sailed across the sea,
    It filled our folks with love and hope
    In the new world colony.
    Frobisher, Chief Massasoit,
    The Pilgrims and Champlain,
    They are why we're gathered here
    And singing this refrain.

CHORUS
As the leaves go dancing 'round
and 'round and 'round they play,
In Canada we celebrate
Our Thanksgiving Day.
We celebrate, we celebrate,
We celebrate today,
In Canada we celebrate
Our Thanksgiving Day.
With five, ten, fifteen, twenty
Things inside the horn o'plenty,
Twenty-five, thirty, thirty-five more
To be thankful for.

2.) October paints a land so green
    With yellow, orange and red.
    We take this chance
    To give our thanks
    For family, home and bread.
    An ages-old tradition,
    Still carried on today,
    Our nation's heart
    Will never part,
    If we believe this way.

REPEAT CHORUS
As the leaves. . .
To be thankful for.

FINAL LINE
In Canada
There's so much more
To be thankful for.

Text copyright © 1993 by Krys Val Lewicki
Illustrations copyright © 1993 by Ana Auml

All rights reserved. No part of this publication may be
reproduced, stored in a retrieval system or transmitted in any
form or by any means, electronic, mechanical, photocopying,
recording or otherwise, without the prior written consent
of the publisher or in accordance with copyright law.

Napoleon Publishing gratefully acknowledges the support of the
Department of the Secretary of State of Canada
A Canada Project 125

Napoleon Publishing
Toronto, Ontario, Canada

Cover and book design by
Pamela Kinney

First Printing   1993
Second Printing   1994
Third Printing   1995

Printed in Canada

Canadian Cataloguing in Publication Data

  Lewicki, Krys Val
      Thanksgiving Day in Canada

ISBN 0-929141-18-0 (bound)   ISBN 0-929141-36-9 (pbk.)

1. Thanksgiving Day - Juvenile literature
I. Auml, Ana.   II. Title

GT4975.L49 1993   j394.2'683   C93-093250-1

PHOTO: AUML

Ana Auml

Ana was born in Uruguay but has lived in Toronto since arriving in Canada in 1964. She has travelled extensively throughout Europe and speaks fluent Spanish and Polish. After completing art studies at the Art Centre at Central Technical, she began a career as a professional photographer, specializing in fashion, promotional and art photography. At the same time, she was stretching her artistic skills by working in theatre and film. Ana has also designed jewellery and worked in film animation. *Thanksgiving Day in Canada* is the second book which she has illustrated for children, the first being *Jennifer has Two Daddies*.

PHOTO: AUML

Krys Val Lewicki

Krys was born in England, where he began his career as a performer at the age of three on Radio Free Europe. Since moving to Toronto at the age of six, Krys has worked extensively with children, as a Cub and Scout Counselor, an entertainer and an athletic coach. A songwriter, musician and actor, Krys has toured all of Canada, made many recordings and appeared often on radio and in television and film. In 1991, he was included in the book *Profiles of Canada's Pop Music Pioneers*. As a writer, he has published *Verdigris*, a book of poems, and his work has been included in an anthology of new international poets. *Thanksgiving Day in Canada* is his first children's book.

Krys and Ana would like to give special thanks to the following people who gave them support and encouragement with the Thanksgiving Day project: Kathy Heal, Marybeth Macdonald, Carolyn Taylor, Allen Morgan, Sylvia McConnell, Mike Hines, Jesse Flis MP, Colène Comeau, Maria Tiley, Patrick Boyer MP, Mary Harhai-Nebesio, Kathleen Sheldon, Steve Harhai, Patricia Boulter, Patrick Niewiadomski, Annette Harhay, Alan Boulter, Lesia Chudoba, Taissa Chudoba, Robert Chudoba, Bohdan Chudoba, Bon Bon and Josie.